ON THE
BODY

Michael G. Whitepak
5/20/02

CARLO MARIA MARTINI

ON THE
BODY

A CONTEMPORARY THEOLOGY
OF THE HUMAN PERSON

Translated by
Rosanna M. Giammanco Frongia, Ph.D.

A Crossroad Book
The Crossroad Publishing Company
New York

The Crossroad Publishing Company
481 Eighth Avenue, New York, NY 10001

Original Edition: *Sul Corpo,* published by ITL spa, Milan, 2000
Copyright © 2000 by ITL spa, 20124, Milan
English translation copyright © 2001 by The Crossroad Publishing Company

Scripture quotations contained herein are from the New Revised Standard Version of the Bible, copyright © 1989, 1995 by the Division of Christian Education of the National Council of the Churches of Christ in the United States of America, and are used by permission. All rights reserved.

Printed in the United States of America

Library of Congress Cataloging-in-Publication Data

Martini, Carlo Maria, 1927-
   [Sul corpo. English]
   On the body : a contemporary theology of the human person / by Carlo Maria Martini ; translated by Rosanna M. Giammanco Frongia.
   ISBN 0-8245-1892-6
   1. Body, Human – Religious aspects – Catholic Church. 2. Catholic Church – Doctrines. I. Title.
   BX1795.B63 M27 2001
   233'.5 – dc21

                                        00-012975

1   2   3   4   5   6   7   8   9   10   06   05   04   03   02   01

CONTENTS

PREFACE

As my twentieth year as bishop of Milan draws to a close and I enter my seventy-third year, I offer this book that I began in February of 1998. At the time, I believed that my age and my sufficiently long experience had qualified me to look back and draw some reflections on the all-important subject of the body.

While my heavy load of pastoral commitments prevented me from finishing the book earlier, it is also true that one's reflections on subjects such as these can never be complete.

As I was writing these pages, I realized how very little I could say on the subject and how much still remains to be said and clarified. Although I received much help and suggestions from experts and friends, I know that this work is woefully incomplete.

Nevertheless, I would like to attempt to write something about the complex reality that is the human body, in which and around which every-thing happens, and which is the subject of so many theories, conflicting attitudes, and arguments.

What does it mean to say that we are a being with a body, that we are a living, thinking body? Does our time in history have something new to contribute to the subject of the body's tribulations and dynamics? Also, what kind of relationship is there between the body and the life of the "spirit," with life after death?

These are some of the questions that I allow to grow inside me, not to find an answer for each and every one but rather to reflect on them out loud as is suitable for an anniversary, when memories converge and become wisdom.

I chose to write this book as a series of notes, comments, and maxims. I thought this was a more appropriate genre than a research paper or exegesis. Here I present brief thoughts about such themes as the healthy body and the sick body, the cult of the body, the body in its sexual specificity, the sacramental journey of the human body, and the body's future. These reflections are intended to provoke thought.

The reader who wishes a more thorough exposition might want to consult catechisms or theological-moral treatises. My purpose was to invite readers to reflect as well as to free themselves from the self-referential cult of the body.

I was moved to write these pages by the words of St. Paul that like an *inner fire* at once spur me on and comfort me: "The body is meant not for fornication but for the Lord, and the Lord for the body" (1 Cor. 6:13).

+ CARLO MARIA CARDINAL MARTINI

HEALTH AND SICKNESS

◆

Once we learn to overcome a possessive, self-enclosed vision of earthly goods, we also learn to believe and hope beyond the vanishing of those goods, health included.

TAKING CARE OF OUR BODY is no longer purely for aesthetic enjoyment as it was for the ancient Greeks, nor is it a pleasure restricted to the few as in ancient Rome. It has become a mass phenomenon.

A *healthy body at all costs*

What we won't do for our body's well-being! It would be safe to say that we obsess about our bodies.

I walk the streets and feel the stare of billboards and ads that promise me "well-being." Drugstores sell products of all kinds to tone our body, improve performance, and give us a youthful appearance. Newspaper stands sell magazines that tell us how to improve our health, lose weight, and become fit. The number of gyms, fitness centers, and spas keeps increasing; sporting goods stores sell expensive sneakers, fitness apparel, and expensive gear for all kinds of sports and exercise.

Why? Because it all makes us *feel good.*

The religion of the body

Truly, health and the search for a pleasing appearance are akin to a form of religion: like religion, they have their devotions, paths of ascent, and forms of sacrifice. We'll do anything to have a beautiful, healthy, desirable body. We'll even lose our soul for our body!

I am reminded here of Sirach, who wrote, "There is no wealth better than health of body" but immediately added, "and no gladness above joy of heart" (30:16). No doubt an important afterthought.

Health and salvation

Now more than ever, the body has become the focus of attention, almost an object of worship.

This is probably a reaction to a lack of appreciation for the body in the past (but who can read the mind of our ancestors?), so that today we value only health and fitness, even mistaking them for "salvation."

While in former times the term "healthy" was used primarily, or at least, in reference to the soul's health (in Latin, *salus* means both health and salvation), today it means only physical health. And we often

14

pursue it with the same degree of anxiety that we put into seeking and desiring salvation.

The health "shrines"

What happens when I think I am about to lose my physical well-being, my fitness?

I am seized by fear as if for the loss of a good that I consider inalienable. For this reason, I turn to shrines and sacred rituals intended for the recovery of health, beauty, strength, and youth.

These shrines have their own sacred vestments (the doctor's scrubs); their processions (the chief physician and his assistants); their liturgies (their initiatory and mysterious language); their prescriptions and their interdicts.

Nor am I overly surprised by all of this. I accept the advantages of this state of affairs and hope in its benefits, though I also ask myself what perception of the human being and the human body this entails.

All-powerful technology

It appears that our own age is finally reaching what men and women have always legitimately aspired to, the lasting, gratifying wellness of the body.

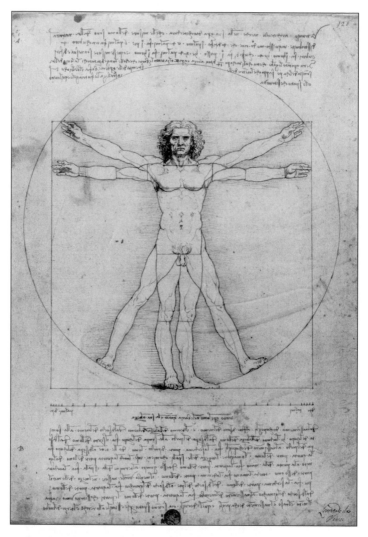

Leonardo da Vinci (1452–1519). Drawing of ideal proportions of the human figure according to Vitruvius's first-century A.D. treatise "De Architectura," ca. 1492. Called "Vitruvian Man." Courtesy: Alinari/Art Resource, NY

While it is true that in all epochs human beings spontaneously sought to remain healthy, today they believe they have the means to be healthy all the time. We have invented sophisticated instruments to examine, preserve, and restore our body's health.

Sometimes we even think that this technology is so powerful as to be almost omnipotent. For this reason, we are upset and incredulous when a doctor cannot find the right cure or a surgeon cannot promise a swift and sure recovery. We are convinced that there must be a solution to our physical ills, if not at home, certainly in other countries, in France, Switzerland, maybe even Australia: someone must have the right drug; someone must know the life-saving surgical procedure!

And if something is not available today, it will surely be within our reach tomorrow: it is just a matter of waiting for the next advance in research or in applied technology. To survive, all we have to do is "hang in there."

The body is no longer silent

When we are healthy, our body is quiet, a silence that is shattered when we fall ill or when we feel physical pain.

Forced to stay in bed, I feel the constraints of time because I have to put my projects on hold; I feel the constraints of space because I cannot move, I cannot meet the people I want to meet.

Sickness is not just "a noise of organs" as someone has written; it is also a noise of thoughts that come to us furiously and torment us: thoughts about my being useless and unable to work, about my fear of being a burden to others, about my refusal to be served or assisted.

Sometimes I am seized by a fear of the future in which I see only darkness; at other times, I feel I am not receiving proper care. Loneliness, physical pain, irritability, disappointment, the difficulty of human interaction—I am disturbed by all this, and these predicaments reveal a part of me I did not know existed.

The positive, spontaneous flow of life has been blocked, and my first impulse is to distrust everyone, myself included.

A dividing line

Sickness takes us back to what is essential: it reveals the roots of a despairing evil and prods us to re-examine everything that we have lived for and still live for.

For as long as we are well, we have no need to read our body.

Thus, illness can become an accuser, a biased prosecutor: What did I do wrong? Why did it have to happen to me? And so illness works as a dividing line. It creates a diabolical place that can destroy me unless I can make sense of it.

Although it's always difficult to live through pain and sickness, it is doubly so when we can make no sense out of our experience.

A serious case

When we are sick, we are forced to reflect on our existence, to rethink the image we had formed of ourselves back when we were healthy and in good shape.

Thus, we experience differently our own corporality—our bodiliness—and the frailty of the human condition, of being creatures, to the point of questioning everything, even asking ourselves whether life is worth living when, after all, we must all die.

This is why the sick need comforting and spiritual support. I will touch upon this subject again when I discuss the sacraments, in particular, the anointing of the sick.

The servant rebels

Sickness is something that affects our flesh; it is an event that makes us notice our body's powerful needs and its cries for help. When we were healthy, the body was quiet and discreet, a dedicated servant.

Now that it's sick, the body is like a rebellious servant demanding to be waited upon, which brings me to ask: What is my body?

Suddenly, this life that I instinctively believed I would experience as pleasure, possession, and achievement, has become an experience of hardship, sorrow, and failure.

I now understand I am not my own master, nor the master of my body or my destiny. I am not even master of my end, because "the body is meant for the Lord" (1 Cor. 6:13).

Sickness is part of life

Sickness is part of life, not like growth or gratification, but more like an interruption, a suspension, a burden, a nuisance even. Far from being an accident, it reveals to us the normal, limited condition of all human satisfaction. Sickness defines me as a fragile, weak, uncertain, and needy being.

Sickness clearly reveals what is hidden in me even when I am healthy, and I fear it because I am loath to see my limitations and my weak points revealed.

The crucial knot

Some illnesses in particular, what we refer to as "incurable diseases," are harbingers of our death and remind us that we shall all die. They anticipate one of life's crucial moments, an event we otherwise refuse to think about and usually don't dwell upon when the body is mute and compliant.

We are not prepared to face the last stretch of our earthly existence. Although we might be willing to climb this steep, challenging mountain, we cannot resign ourselves to the fact that we must take a final leap to reach the top. Or we would like to be able to own this instant, to "pull the plug" when we are ready. We resist throwing ourselves into the hands of God.

What unites all men and women is the fear of death, this crucial knot, this brutal, inescapable fact.

While it is true that fear of death can help us to survive insofar as it marshals the instincts of self-preservation and resistance—as in the case of war or concentration camp survivors—it is also true that it is difficult to control, for it surges instinctively and is stronger than we are. Even Jesus experienced fear. Our only remedy is prayer: "My Father, if this is possible, let this cup pass from me; yet not what I want, but what you want" (Matt. 26:39).

The limits of medical science

Today when we are sick we are usually consigned into the hands of physicians, of medicine, of technology. But this is not enough nor can it be enough, for when we are sick we need an interpretation of our condition as a patient, and medicine cannot provide it.

Medicine is concerned with treating disease and postponing death, sometimes for an indefinite period. Yet by doing so, sometimes we run the risk that we will no longer have a space in which to come to terms with the meaning of our illness.

We must never forget that technology has to do with means, and that when we choose to treat it as an end, we make an idol out of it.

Sick persons may want to know the severity of their condition. Several years ago a priest who was sick with cancer and was able to secretly read his diagnosis wrote that he was happy to know what

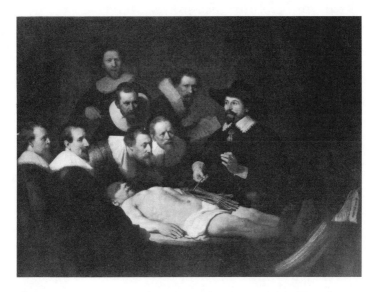

Rembrandt van Rijn (1606–1669). *The Anatomy Lesson of Dr. Nicholas Tulp*. 1632. Oil on canvas. Mauritshuis, The Hague, The Netherlands. Courtesy: Giraudon/Art Resource, NY

the doctors knew about him. He felt it was his right to know, for he wanted with all his strength to be conscious that he was facing death.

A call for help, for love, for meaning

Sickness is not simply a medical problem: it is a call for help, for love, and for meaning.

Many times during his public life, Jesus submitted to the radical pleas of sick people.

Sick persons who receive help can become a powerful attraction, as they speak from their heart about long-ignored, neglected feelings of courage, hope, endurance, and the refusal to give in.

The chronically ill in particular experience the loss of people willing to share their tribulations. This is a serious flaw in a society such as ours that is dominated by a "culture of health."

Open your eyes

Physical pain can become an opportunity for interaction instead of a loss of meaning, an opportunity for sharing instead of isolation, an opportunity for accepting our own differences and those of others.

Again, suffering can be an opportunity for conversion. Our eyes open onto a horizon that can give meaning even to an existence filled with sickness and death, because our life is not a journey toward nothingness, but a journey toward the Lord who is coming to meet us.

My experience with the sick

In my twenty years as bishop, I've had numerous opportunities to visit the sick, both in the hospital and in their homes.

I recall the faces of young, very young sick people, and those of sick elderly men and women. I have experienced firsthand how pain can awaken the soul, a being that otherwise might not even be aware of its own invaluable existence.

I have also discovered that those who are "healthy" are tempted to neglect many of life's meanings.

Truly, there are places in the human heart that only pain can bring to light!

The sick whom I met or who wrote to me—and they are many—have enriched my life by sharing with me their hopes, their faith, and their infinite patience.

Undoubtedly, I have received much more than I intended to give in my visits or my letters to the sick, for from the body of a sick person we can work our way back to an understanding of the authentic body.

Humility

I believe that the most genuine approach to illness should be one of humility, since we have no way of predicting what will be our reactions, our sensations, or our feelings at the time of our trial.

Sooner or later, this trial too will be at our door. "Father ... do not bring us to the time of trial" (Matt. 6:13).

Health and prayer

Is there a correlation between health and prayer? I believe there is, certainly in the sense that many of our prayers, including the Psalms and the Gospels, are really petitions about the health of our body. Like the leper, we often say: "If you choose, you can make me clean" (Mark 1:40), or like the blind man: "My teacher, let me see again" (Mark 10:51). But I would also like to stress that prayer, when practiced regularly, promotes inner peace, composure, good spirits, and a positive temperament that is a factor in our well-being. Of course, we should pray because we enjoy conversing with God and not to seek these results.

Prayer and sickness

Praying when we are sick is more difficult, both on account of the physical discomfort we experience and because our faith is on trial. Yet it is precisely for this reason that illness can inspire in us a more mystical, more elemental prayer. For only then can we suffer together with Jesus, in the awareness of "completing what is lacking in Christ's afflictions for the sake of his body, that is, the church" (Col. 1:24).

WHAT IS THE BODY?

◆

Rarely does one live in one's body
as if in a temporary dwelling.

—St. Basil of Caesarea

THROUGHOUT HISTORY, humankind has treated the body with suspicion and ambiguity, and it is difficult to harmonize in theory and practice the many interpretations of it that exist.

Which body?

"Which" body is receiving so much interest today? What is the body, and what is its use?

These questions have always been open-ended, just as the human being, the questioner, is open-ended.

Unless we answer them, we shall remain captive to one specific, contemporary idea of the body and the pressing needs and fashions derived from such a conception.

What we need is a yardstick, a benchmark, a meaning.

Are we perhaps running the risk of dismembering, fragmenting the body, and thus losing its overall meaning? Observe, in this respect, the advertising images of products targeted to specific parts of the body, or even the subdivision of medicine into a myriad of specialized sectors.

Do we also perhaps run the risk that an obsessive attention to our own individual body might undermine our relationships with others?

Who am I?

In general, a body is any object that the eye and the touch can perceive.

Obviously, when we talk about the human body this definition is insufficient, unless we are talking about a lifeless body.

Far from being a mere object, our body is first and foremost a subject; and it is a subject not just of touch and sight, but of all our actions and passions.

Before any kind of reflection, the reality of the body is thrust into the world: at the moment of its birth, the baby's body differentiates itself from the mother's: it becomes an object of care and of love; it meets other bodies, and so finally recognizes itself.

Who am I? The answer I give to this question has to do with the way in which I understand my body, which is the place where I first come to know myself as well as others.

Many secret voices

Human beings have always asked questions about ourselves and our bodies. Though it is *my* body, I can reflect upon it as if it were alien to me. It seems as if my body has many secret voices, each one eager to tell me something about my body and everything else.

Through my body, I live the adventure of being born and dying; I experience growth and decay, eating, encounters, love. My history, my desires, my joys and my sorrows, my hopes and my expectations, my disappointments, my victories, and my wounds... they are all inscribed in my flesh.

For this reason, I am tempted to say, "I am my body," though in effect, I feel that what I am truly saying is, "I have a body." And this creates confusion.

An enigma

This body that defines me at the same time restricts me. It is always at the center of my horizon of action and thought; at the same time, I perceive that it connects me to what is "beyond."

The body is something inside of which I find myself, something that I notice, that I touch and I see, that I can measure and differentiate from another body. But as soon as I try to understand it further, the difficulties begin.

Strangely, I am more clearly aware of spirit, something I can neither see nor touch, yet something I am keenly aware of because when it is present the body is alive, swift, and keen, and when it fails, it is pale and lifeless.

The body occupies space, at least for an unknown stretch of time. Then it dissolves and becomes one with surrounding matter. While I am alive, I am where my body is, although my heart knows that it *also* lives elsewhere, where its object of longing and love resides.

For this reason, the body is always restless and searching. But what does it seek? Its own identity? Its own truth? It is truly a riddle!

The coincidence of opposites

My body places me in a certain location in space and time, separating me from others or uniting me with them. It moves and it stops, it is attracted and repelled, it turns thought on and off.

Thus, the body is in a sense a coincidence of opposites. It does everything, yet it is not everything; it is only one body, yet it needs every body; it exists now, yet it did not exist before and will not exist later; it knows what is good and beautiful, and also what is ugly and dangerous.

Body and spirit

Implicitly, almost spontaneously, we think of the body as being opposed to *spirit,* and in a sense this is correct.

More to the point, spirit is the *breath,* the life of the body: it makes the body live and makes it live in a certain way. It is spirit that makes the body what it is, that marks it and distinguishes it.

What I can say is that my body, and my face in particular, are like the outline and the history of my spirit.

When we meet someone who is good, generous, devoted to others, meek, of generous heart, capable of forgiveness, we realize that that person's face— even if it is more wrinkled than the face of Mother Teresa of Calcutta—is beautiful. For in it shines true beauty, luminous, inner, spiritual beauty that attracts us by radiating joy, serenity, harmony, and peace.

Sympathy and suspicion

A peaceful relationship with our body is not at all to be taken for granted: often, we treat it with both sympathy and suspicion at once. We exalt it yet also belittle it, treating it as an absolute value but also as a cage of the spirit, as the realm of need and a source of pain.

Spiritualism

From its inception, our Western culture has interpreted the "body" in opposition to the "soul."

The body is what we share with all the other beings and creatures on earth, while the soul is what differentiates us as human beings.

Soul is our vital, incorruptible part endowed with intelligence and freedom, while the body is our mortal, corruptible part, subjected to passions and needs.

For Socrates, death was simply the separation of the soul from the body: not only could the soul survive without the body, but it behooved us to keep it early on as far removed from the body as possible (*Phaedo* 64a).

Plato, on the other hand, believed that the soul was united to the body only by accident. He was convinced that the body—*soma* in Greek—was the grave (*sema*) of the soul, a prison from which it had to escape. While waiting for death to permanently release it from the body, the soul had to subdue the body and lead it up the path of ascent.

Materialism

The materialistic conception is, of course, juxtaposed to the spiritualistic one that looks down on the body. According to Epicurus (*Fragment* 130.414), the soul was to be explained mechanically; it was the movement of the body, both the body and its movements being holy.

Though extreme and oversimplified, these two positions still survive, together with other, more nuanced and complex views. In any case, the Western way of understanding the human being is based on these two opposite conceptions with all their later variants and explanations.

The body and the Bible

According to Sacred Scripture, the human being is a whole and the human body is at once part of earth and of heaven. It is clay come alive by God's breath of life, "The Lord God formed man from the dust of the ground, and breathed into his nostrils the breath of life; and the man became a living being" (Gen. 2:7).

We usually refer to the human body as "flesh"—*basar* in Hebrew—flesh that lives for the "spirit," which is *ruah* in Hebrew.

The human being is fashioned of earth and of life-giving breath, and both come from God and were created by God's Word. While it is said that each living being was created "according to its species," there is no mention of the species to which human beings might belong. For they belong to the divine species, having been created "in his image and likeness" (see Gen. 1:26).

Clay and breath are thus bound together in a state of tension because the spirit needs the flesh to express itself, and the flesh, the body, cannot transcend itself without the breath of life.

The body in Christianity

We know that from the very beginning Christianity had to come to terms with the dominant Greek worldview. Although adopting some of the latter's elements, Christianity held fast to the Bible's positive vision of the body, even in the midst of many opposing currents.

Undoubtedly, the biblical approach was also subjected to the influence of negative conceptions such as those of Origen, Gregory of Nyssa, Jerome, and Augustine; these conditioned to some extent Christianity's approach to the body in later centuries.

In any case, a pessimistic understanding of the body was always counterbalanced by an unquestionable truth: the revelation that the human being is beautiful indeed (see Gen. 1:31), that the body comes from God, that it is made in God's image and likeness, and that the Word became flesh. That flesh, in the words of Tertullian, is the cornerstone of salvation: *caro salutis cardo*.

The mystery of Incarnation

The Word became flesh, and this event ushered in a totally new vision of the body. By taking on our mortal flesh, the Son of God wanted to share in our weakness, in our frailty, a frailty that no longer obscures the beauty of our body.

For just as the body of Jesus is a revelation of glory, the Invisible made visible, the narration of God among humankind, so our body, a totality comprised of flesh and spirit, is meant to be a mirror in which divine beauty is reflected.

Thus, we can say that because of the mystery of Incarnation that is completed in the mystery of Resurrection, the body and the state of corporality are central to Christianity.

The body of Christ, offered on our behalf, is at the heart of Christian life and thought. For this reason, St. Paul writes that our body becomes our *"reasonable* act of worship" (from the Greek *loghikos,* having to do with our innermost reason for being), "holy and pleasing to God" (see Rom. 12:1 NIV). No longer captive to systems of thought that devalue the body, we live it in the belief that we belong to Christ just as Christ belongs to us.

A Note

Of course, flesh remains the weak, mortal aspect of the human being.

This unavoidable fact is at the core of our negative views of the term: in fact, to trust in the "flesh," to live according to the "flesh," means to withdraw into ourselves, inside our limitations, using them as tools of defense as well as attack.

We are reminded, in contrast, of the medieval wisdom that *homo habet animam, sed est corpus:* though we *have* a soul, we *are* a body—dust, earth.

Today we are fully aware that we have a body, but maybe we have forgotten that the body has a soul.

The body speaks

What should we say then about the body?

I confess my embarrassment. I am surprised to realize that our body *speaks*, and that it listens because every other body speaks to it.

Our body is intimately marked by the word, which is its differentiating quality and which gives it its human dignity. Again, our body speaks not only with words but also with its very mode of being.

Now this is truly the problem: how to live one's body, for it can either lose itself or save itself, it can live to die or it can live to live.

What I would like to know about the body is the *word that is not spoken*, the word that is inscribed in it, that speaks its meaning and its destiny. Because unless we understand this word we destroy our body by making it into an absolute, an idol, a void to which we sacrifice our life.

We shall try to listen to what the body is saying, to the word that *is* the body. For we become the interpretation we give of our own body.

OTHERNESS AND SEXUALITY

◆

One day Zeus, wanting to punish man without destroying him, cut him in two. Since then, each of us is like the symbol of a man, a half looking for the other half, for its corresponding symbol.

—Plato, *Symposium*, XVI

So God created humankind in his image, in the image of God he created them; male and female he created them.

—Genesis 1:27

THE GREEK MYTH narrated by Plato of a round, perfect man split in two by Zeus, resulting in two halves always in search of each other, contains a truth that we experience over and over again: that the body is like a word that has been left unspoken; it is an incomplete reality that points to something else.

This pointing is more than just a need for physical completeness, because it has to do with all of our bodily being, in relation to what is other than ourselves.

"... male and female he created them"

In the first chapter of Genesis the Bible stresses that the body of man and woman was created in the *image and likeness of God, also insofar as they were male and female:* "Let us make humankind in our image, according to our likeness.... So God created humankind in his image; in the image of God he created them; male and female he created them" (Gen. 1:26–27).

This revelation is fundamental if we want to understand the body and how it becomes itself.

Michelangelo. *The Creation of Eve.*
Courtesy: Alinari/Art Resource, NY

"... *flesh of my flesh*"

There is a second biblical story that explains the body: "Then the Lord God said: 'It is not good that the man should be alone. . . . ' So the Lord God caused a deep sleep to fall upon the man, and he slept; then he took one of his ribs and closed up its place with flesh. And the rib that the Lord God had taken from the man he made into a woman and brought her to the man. Then the man said, 'This at last is bone of my bones and flesh of my flesh' " (Gen. 2:18, 21–23).

Adam was sleeping! He came back to life when Eve, his other part, was born from the wound in his heart. He woke up with an exclamation of joy and wonder and recognized himself in the *otherness of the woman.* Man rejoices because he is no longer alone, because he has discovered someone who is other than himself.

The word of the human body

These two biblical texts answer a crucial question about the body.

My body has a precise word inscribed in it: this word is the *other;* it is a calling for the other; the body becomes itself in the face of the other, by relating to the other.

But the other is a mystery that cannot be reduced to an analogy or simplified by a comparison; if I want to own it, it is no longer the "other" and I am left alone, with no one else. The sex difference makes man and woman unfinished in themselves, each definable only with reference to the other.

There is no space here for lovely Narcissus, who looks at his reflection in the water: for by looking at his own image, all he can do is drown.

The implications of this biblical revelation are manifold.

The other speaks the Other

The word inscribed in the body, the other, speaks of the Other; it speaks of God, of what is holy: "Sanctify yourselves therefore, and be holy, for I am holy" (Lev. 11:44), for to be holy means "to be different, to be other with respect to all others." The body is for the Other, for the Lord (see 1 Cor. 6:13).

My body is called to live in a different way, one that is proper to God, to God's beauty, so that it may be a reflection of the glory of God, as "God's temple" (1 Cor. 3:16).

God's seal

In the Bible, the man-woman couple is not meant to be simply a means for the preservation of the species, as is the case for the other animals. Insofar as it was called to become the image and likeness of God, it expresses in a bodily, tangible way the face of God, which is Love.

We could say that sexual otherness *forces* men and women to be like God, in the sense of having to place themselves in a relationship of sympathy, of synergy, of communion, of fruitfulness.

From this fact arises the Christian's profound respect for the body and for sexuality, whose dignity must never be distorted or sold short. Hence, sexuality can be neither "unruly" nor "unreasonable": it has a meaning, a direction, rules, and boundaries.

It is precisely in the reciprocal love of man and woman, a love that is neither self-enclosed nor self-sufficient, but open to the God who wants to be one with man and woman, that the body, bearing as it does the seal of God, leads us back to God.

For I exist only if I am loved, and I exist only if I love. Truly, love is that divine element that allows our body to exist.

Therefore, sex contains a sublime word of love

that completes the person in the likeness of God, whose Holiness is Love.

Hence, a sexuality that does not discover the word inscribed in the body, but reduces the body to non-sense, despising and disrespecting it, empties it of meaning.

For whether the body has a meaning or not depends on the love that one gives.

By giving of ourselves, we promote freedom, but when we do not give of ourselves and only look to ourselves, we hinder and destroy freedom.

Sexuality and freedom

Sexuality is a gift from God, energy that is available to all of us. How we use it is left up to us.

If I have a container with a hundred cards with writing on them, I can put on a blindfold and randomly take out whatever card my hand happens to touch; though the game may be fun, I'm expressing neither intelligence nor freedom.

Or I could take out those cards, put the words in order, and use them to write an essay.

It is the same material, but it gives different results depending on whether it is used randomly or with good intent.

"Freedom" is an ambiguous word. The body of the man and of the woman is the link between necessity and freedom. It is beyond instinct.

Freedom and instinct

Of necessity, animals are ruled by instinct that moves them in a certain direction.

On the other hand, the human body is inhabited by reasonable freedom; it is possibility and openness.

For the Christian, to be free means to live one's body with the capacity of using it for a loving purpose. It does not mean doing what we like or only what we must. It means doing what pleases God, for I want to please those who love me and whom I love.

Thus, Christian freedom is not the freedom of the playboy who is a slave to his every impulse. Nor is it the freedom of the Stoic who denies all impulses. It is, rather, the freedom to love and to be the master of one's own body. It is a freedom best expressed by achieving "self-control" (see Gal. 5:22).

In the Christian worldview, the beauty and harmony of sexuality are an art to be learned, like poetry or painting or music. Being able to relate to another allows us to direct our impulses freely, according to the Lord's inspiration, rather than letting them act blindly, randomly, or clumsily.

We must learn to live our sexuality as an expression of love and of communion with God.

The body as boundary

The body, which attracts the other and vice versa, also marks a *boundary*.

From the dawn of human history, men and women have lived this boundary as a place of death rather than of life, of defense and attack rather than acceptance, of conformity rather than freedom, of monotonous narcissism rather than harmony with others.

Sexuality is a boundary that brings us back to the other, to someone who is other than myself. It is the most obvious place that we can be either "against" or "for" the other: it is where life is at stake.

While breathing, drinking, and eating have to do with my body, exercising my sexuality has to do with the other and makes me be *for* the other; it sets up a radical, though not automatic, separation and attraction with respect to the other.

I am known to the other

All of us, men and women, know ourselves by reflecting upon ourselves, though there are some aspects of our being that are known only to the other, that only a woman can know about a man and vice versa.

Thus, none of us can claim to be capable of self-definition: we must allow ourselves to be helped by the perception that the other has of us.

Complementary, not different

To say that there is a difference between the male and female sex is not entirely correct.

"Difference" means a relationship between non-equals, where someone has or is more than the other.

Nor would I speak of simple diversity, which emphasizes the different characteristics of men and women; "integration" might be a more appropriate word.

But perhaps the most suitable term is "complementarity," which denotes a correlated diversity between two individuals who complete each other into a whole.

Being complementary allows us to rejoice in the good of the other. Our difference becomes a principle of sharing, of reciprocal giving and accepting, of reciprocal service, and fills our love with humility, respect, faithfulness, and reverence.

God's partner

We become what we love; the beloved becomes the vital center of the lover: *amatus fit forma amantis.*

God, being loved, becomes the life of the human being, for according to the Scriptures: "You shall love the Lord your God with all your heart, and with all your soul, and with all your might" (Deut. 6:5), with all your life and all your intelligence.

Sexuality marks our body with the sign of this splendid plan: I am God's partner; God is my own identity.

In the Bible, the relationship between man and woman is an image of the relationship between God and the human being. In this sense, "femaleness becomes the symbol of all humanity" (*Mulieris Dignitatem* 25): to be the bride of God, to be like God insofar as we have been called to respond to God's love for us, is human destiny.

We find this conjugal aspect of love in many pages of the Scriptures, particularly in the Song of Songs, in the prophet Hosea, and in Revelation.

Whether man or woman, we are made to love God absolutely, as God's sole partner in the fullest sense of the word.

Thus, passionate, faithful love, the love that joins a man and a woman, binding them into one flesh—in the words of Genesis 2:24—is a reflection of the love that led God to be united to the human species, to be one flesh with humankind, in Jesus. And likewise, we can say, "But anyone united to the Lord becomes one spirit with him" (1 Cor. 6:17).

Sexuality and responsibility

When the church talks about sexuality, we expect it to issue rules and prohibitions. Actually, the church is merely interpreting the common wisdom of humanity in the light of the Gospel.

Even a nonreligious morality that is neither reductive nor prejudiced, but honestly seeks the full meaning of the human being in the world, must be able to indicate what is sexually allowed and what is forbidden, along with the meaning of sexuality and how it can be fulfilled.

These rules imply values and meanings; they are designed to raise our awareness and make us understand what gives true happiness. Since the dawn of history, human society, in its wisdom, has always understood that without prohibitions there can be no true expression of joy, and that some taboos are important, provided they are reasonable.

Those familiar with the church's teaching on sexuality know that the church's intent is fundamentally to *educate*. Reflecting on human experience and taking its inspiration from the Word of God, the church advocates the full truth of human sexuality, a truth that sheds light on the very needs and responsibilities that are built into the structure of human sexuality.

Thus, the church sets forth a doctrine and an ethic that promote human development, an ethic about sexual issues that is rooted in the very meaning of "responsibility" and its implications.

The classic rule

The classic rule about sexuality is very simple. The gratification we receive from sexual acts acquires a true human meaning when it is directed to the loving union of a man and a woman who are bound to each other by total, reciprocal fidelity and who are open to procreation.

Whatever falls outside of this rule falls outside of the Christian order.

As a result, there are a multitude of actions, gestures, thoughts, and desires that either go in the right direction or deviate in varying degrees from the rule.

Some thoughts or actions even exclude conjugal union and either withdraw one into oneself or use the other merely as a tool for one's own self-centeredness. These are the most distressing perversions.

A whole casuistry of sexual morality has developed out of these principles, but we shall not go into it here.

I would like to point out, however, that not every "disorder" is a sin in the theological and religious meaning of the term. In order for it to constitute a sin, the author must be conscious that his or her free, optional gesture seriously upsets the inner balance and relational quality of a properly formed sexuality, thus disturbing its role of submission to God's design for human happiness.

I am convinced that often these deviations from the basic rule are due more to superficiality, to a lazy, disorderly sensuality, to fickle attraction, or to a deep-seated ignorance of the true order and direction of sexuality than to a true intent to sin. Thus, it is important to engage in a process, even gradual, to clarify these issues with the aim of achieving self-mastery. In this respect, the advice of a mature person and the sacrament of reconciliation will be of great help.

Sexual consumerism

We note with sorrow that consumerism has reduced sex to a commodity, using it even for exchange or as a marketing tool. Sexuality cannot and must not be degraded to the level of an object or an idol, that is, an image. These days, the body, its exterior beauty and pleasing it, are at the center of culture. But because ours is a culture of the "image," not of the spirit, it cannot grasp the deeper and truer dimension of the body.

Chastity

As Karol Wojtyla, now Pope John Paul II, wrote in *Love and Responsibility,* chastity is "a transparent attitude with respect to an individual of the opposite sex." On the contrary, contemporary culture claims that we must acknowledge and satisfy all our psychophysical and psychosomatic drives, in the belief that controlling one's sexuality might lead to excessive tension and nervous disorders. Conversely, chastity is order, balance, mastery, and harmony.

Many people say: "This is my body, and I'll do whatever I want with it. While I am responsible for outward actions that may harm others, what I do to my body is my own business." This type of talk contradicts everything we said about the body and its relational quality.

Unfortunately, the sensual and hedonistic atmosphere that prevails in the press, on TV, at the movies does have an effect. Even many Christians who in principle accept God's primacy over the body look too casually and easily at newspapers, magazines, films, and shows of all kinds, deriving from it a guilty superficiality that mars the beauty of chastity.

The beauty of chastity

As a matter of fact, chastity is a beautiful way of life that must be considered in the light of love's beauty.

Rather than despising the body, chastity allows us to channel its energies, diverting them from self-centeredness toward service to others.

While it is true that the root of the word "chastity" recalls "austerity," "holding in check," in a positive sense chastity teaches us the discipline of the heart, of the eye, of language, of all our senses. All of this yields ease of movement, liberty, harmony, and peace. Far from being negative, chastity is true mastery of the self; in making this choice, we acknowledge that Jesus is master of our bodies and our lives. On this subject, St. Paul has said the words that first moved me to write this book, words that are like fire: "The body is meant not for fornication but for the Lord, and the Lord for the body" (1 Cor. 6:13).

Chastity makes us live our body in the freedom of the Spirit, a freedom that begets love, joy, peace, patience, benevolence, moderation, self-control, courtesy, meekness, forbearance (see Gal. 5:22). The saying that "there is greater joy in sacrifice" is true in this case as well.

Different life situations

Of course, chastity takes on different meanings and nuances depending on specific life situations.

There is a way of being chaste for married couples and a way of being chaste for the widowed; a way of being chaste for those who for reasons not of their own choosing are single; and yet another way of being chaste for those who have been called to consecrate their virginity to the kingdom.

In particular, there is one way of practicing

chastity for adolescents and young adults. For it is during these years that boys and girls build the ideal foundation of their personality and develop it, just as they work toward integrity and self-control. All of this will have positive effects on the rest of their lives.

Educating oneself to chastity

In discussing sexuality, we cannot just rely on arguments about what is right and what is wrong; for in these matters reason is like a dike that can easily burst.

We must begin from a spiritual intuition that helps us grasp the obligations inherent in the fact that our body belongs to God. Rational arguments, by their very nature, cannot go beyond their own premises and so cannot explore the depths of the person—who may continue to live rationally a life of compromise, deceit, and collusion. Only a spiritual intuition can guide us on the path to chastity—a path that requires that we constantly conquer and subject ourselves to the extraordinary greatness of love.

All of this requires that we be humble, that we pray, that we be bold, and that we persevere. It is a long road toward deliverance.

Chastity is like poverty

Chastity is an education and a training that aims to overcome any mentality that looks to our body and that of another in a possessive, exclusionary way.

It is a sort of evangelical "poverty" because it also applies to food and the luxury goods that mark our consumer society; likewise, it entails a moderate, intelligent use of media such as television.

Chastity and a pure heart

Being pure of heart is an evangelical beatitude— "Blessed are the pure in heart, for they will see God" (Matt. 5:8)—a broader attitude that encompasses chastity.

Being pure of heart can help us discover the primary cause of a lot of confusion in matters of faith.

For when the will becomes weak and relationships with friends are no longer chaste, the heart is not pure and we feel like banal Christians. We do not pray; we feel the need for constant excitement. Such situations are fertile ground for those temptations that could lead to loss of faith.

The fruits of chastity

Chastity is beautiful and produces lovely fruits: the unifying experience of life, freedom from false absolutes, openness toward truth, a disposition to service and dedication, the strength to live, to be a witness, and to proclaim the great values of existence.

An uncomfortable discourse

I realize that talking about Christian chastity is uncomfortable, even paradoxical, in the light of today's lifestyles. Nevertheless, chastity creates a disposition and openness toward an evangelical model of love and freedom.

I believe it is my duty to talk about it, addressing young people in particular.

From birth

An interest in sexuality begins even before birth, as parents tend to think differently about their unborn child depending on its sex.

In any case, it is important to treat children from birth in a way that allows them to perceive their bodies correctly. Educating the child to sexuality is the cornerstone of the whole educational process.

Educating to give selflessly

The transition from adolescence to adulthood is achieved not by becoming intellectually mature, but by learning to develop an altruistic, gratuitous, disinterested love.

A boy and a girl become a man and a woman when they are able to forget themselves for the good of others.

Before that, they are still, psychologically speaking, adolescents or even children.

Such transition does not occur automatically or at random; it is the end result of an education to love that is rooted in the capacity of mastering one's sexual impulses and desires.

Learning to love does not mean being initiated into the techniques of the sexual act or into the search of an enjoyment that is separate from interpersonal union and the possibility of procreation.

Young people and chastity

Committing to a chaste way of life when we are young creates an optimum condition of inner transparency that predisposes us to listen to the Word of God and the suggestions of the Spirit, clearing our mind of dull and heavy thoughts. For this reason, those who have not made a sincere effort to live a chaste life will rarely experience a calling to the religious life.

A chaste youth, on the other hand, will more easily follow any pure inspiration and accept God, overcoming weakness and inertia.

Chastity does not repress desire, nor does it ridicule it or deny it. Instead, it redirects desire at its source, while strengthening a young person's resolve to consider a different, more complex approach to life. Gradually, the youth will come to understand that sexuality cannot be made into a tool, nor can it be forced or wasted: it must be accepted in the context of the meaning that visibly courses through it.

A bold proposal

In my years of episcopal service, I have found that young people are not hostile to a bold proposal to be chaste. Often, they demand it from their teachers, even if they are aware of their own contradictions and of how easy it is to fall into compromise.

Maybe even more than adults, young people perceive that what is at stake is true love and a correct use of this priceless asset that is sexuality. They also worry that they might exhaust the resources nature has given them to help them make the right choices in love.

God's plan

Educating someone to the meaning of sexuality does not just draw from a generic attention to what is human or an emphasis on the findings of human science; it is founded on God's design.

For the body is the House of God, the place where God is manifest, the visible expression of the mystery of the invisible Trinity, which is at once supreme freedom and supreme love: "Do you not know that you are God's temple and that God's Spirit dwells in you?" (1 Cor. 3:16).

THE SACRAMENTS

---◆---

And the Word became flesh and lived among us.
— John 1:14

This is my body, which is given for you.
— Luke 22:19

*The body is meant ... for the Lord,
and the Lord for the body.*

— 1 Corinthians 6:13

The body is meant for the Lord and the Lord for the body.

The reciprocity expressed in the wonderful words of St. Paul is a mystery that broadens our worldview and powerfully releases our body.

"The body is meant for the Lord." It is for the fullness of life, not for destruction: the body is fated to live its love for God both temporally and in eternity.

"The body is meant for the Lord." My heart lives next to him, loves him, recognizes him, and plans my path so that I may reach him and walk with him always.

"The Lord is for the body." The Word, the Son of God, was made flesh, took on a body to be with me and be like me. He chose to join himself to me, give himself to me and show me on earth his eternal love, teaching me how to live with this body of mine as if it were a gift of love. Summarizing his life, Jesus said: "This is my body given for you … do this in memory of me." For two millennia, an immense multitude of men and women has lived in memory of these words.

A Christian body

Christianity is squarely based on the body that Christ took on, for it is the religion of *Logos* made flesh, of the Word that became Man.

The body of Christ is projected on the bodies of Christians as they are dipped in baptismal water; it accompanies the bodies of Christians throughout their lives, until their final illness and death, as a prelude to the resurrection of those same bodies. The body of the Christian is alive precisely because it is connected to the body of the resurrected Christ and becomes part of the greater body of Christ, which is the church.

Therefore, at the center of Christianity is a body that is born, grows, communicates, reproduces itself, suffers, falls ill, is cured, and dies: because the word lives precisely through the body's existence.

This means that all the different stages of my body have a meaning; they have a "word" that refers to it.

This word is uttered by the sacraments of the church.

The sacraments

The sacraments make explicit and articulate the body's unspoken language: they actualize the body's power of communication. Within each sacrament is a word that gives shape, life, and full meaning to things and actions that concern the human body and its path toward God, always with reference to the body of Christ and the body of the church.

The birth and development of the body are linked to baptism, to confirmation, and to reconciliation.

Nourishment and becoming adults are linked to the Eucharist and to holy orders.

Loving and being loved are linked to the sacrament of marriage.

Suffering and death are linked to the sacrament of the anointing of the sick and to the *dies natalis*, death, which is the final baptism.

The resulting picture is a conception of death as a birth into life and the promise of the resurrection and transfiguration of the body.

Baptism, the word of being born

Birth is a traumatic experience, of which only a dim, indirect awareness remains in our consciousness. Be-

71

ing born means being thrown out of our mother's body and into the world.

This experience is at the root of the innate, unconscious feeling of loneliness that every human being feels.

At the same time, it also means to be born to oneself, to come into the light, to exist as a person. For we are born from an other, and in differentiating ourselves from the other, we become ourselves an other.

This otherness is comprised of two meanings. The first is negative: to be detached, separated, alone, alien, radically wounded, other than the source of our life, and to carry our own scars. The second, positive meaning is of being oneself, being other than the other, being active, free subjects who are able to overcome loneliness through communion and love.

Baptism utters the revealed word about our birth. It tells me that I neither come from a meaningless nothing nor do I return to nothing, for I come from God and to God I return. I come from God to be projected into the life and death of God's Son Jesus.

My being born was not only an act of being thrown out, almost expelled. It was also the fruit of an act of love from the other, intending to establish with me a relationship of love. Because we are alive as persons only insofar as we are loved, baptism is my warranty that the love of my parents, who conceived me and welcomed me into the world, is a reflection of that Love that never disappoints.

For in baptism I recognize that I am the other part of God just as God is my other part, just as Eve, born of Adam's wound, is at once other than him and yet totally directed back to him. In baptism, I accept and profess that I am born from the wound of Jesus' love on the cross, from the ribs of the new Adam who sleeps the sleep of death.

Being children in the Son

With baptism, I am told that I am a child of God and that I have within me an inexhaustible source of life.

My parents are not the first absolute parents, but the intermediary of God's love for all humankind, as their Father.

Acknowledging that we are children of God is at the root of our freedom from all parental and social ties: it makes such bonds relative compared to the ultimate status—that of being children in the Son. Such acknowledgment is also at the root of the brotherhood and sisterhood of all men and women, who are all equally called to this condition before God.

Again, baptism is a path on which we walk for the

duration of our lives. Just as we are born to live, so we are baptized to dive deeper and deeper into the freedom of our love for our Father and our brothers and sisters. As we are born, our body leaves our mother's and is delivered to the earth; but in baptism, we are delivered to the Spirit. Thus, our body lives on earth the same life as the Son of God and the fruits of the Spirit (see Gal. 5:22).

Is baptism for adults or for children?

If we look at baptism as a road to be traveled, certainly baptism is for those adults who are capable of making choices. However, if we look at the grace that is innate in the sacrament, clearly newborn babies are already capable of receiving all the love that God has intended for them. In baptism, children are proclaimed free beings, born of love, capable of connecting with the Father and their brothers and sisters. Once children are able to recognize this stupendous reality, their baptism is reaffirmed by their adult conscience.

A communitarian dimension

Baptism is not a private matter, for being born means being thrown into the world of relations that make life possible. Similarly, baptism means being thrown into the community of our Father's children, who have his same Spirit.

Gestures and symbols

With symbolic gestures and words, the rite of baptism celebrates what I have tried to express in a simple, concrete manner. Let us read anew those gestures and symbols, especially as we witness the baptism of a child who is dear to us.

"What name do you want to give this child?" To name a child means to recognize it as having value in and of itself, and equal dignity. To be called means to become aware that we exist as relational subjects. For the more we are called, the more we exist.

For example, there is beauty when I hear my name called in the midst of a faceless crowd, for it means that someone knows me and this helps me to exist as a person.

My name is a reflection of the Name of God; it is sharing in God's glory. If my name is also that of a saint, it links me to that particular story, a promise that I am part of the communion of saints.

Exorcism and the anointing of the baptisand. From the beginning, our name is woven into a history where not everything is good, a history dominated by mistrust, the inability to communicate, fear, selfishness, and aggressiveness. Baptism gives us the certainty that we shall be capable of self-defense, slipping out of these bonds. The rite of exorcism predisposes us to conquer evil with good and to forsake all that is negative.

The oil of our anointing is the same oil that prepares the athlete for combat, for life is a struggle directed to reach the full freedom enjoyed by the children of God; it is a progressive release of our body from everything that enslaves it.

Water. To be submerged in water means to die; to come up again and breathe means to live. Baptism, the immersion in water, is like a dying that we may be reborn into the new life of the Spirit. Just as the people of Israel were freed from Egyptian slavery by walking into the Red Sea on their way to freedom, so through baptism we leave the conditioning of the idols and are ready to conform our life to that of the Son, Jesus.

With the formula "I baptize you in the Name of the Father and of the Son and of the Holy Spirit" we are thrust into the mystery of the Trinity, of the creative and redeeming power of God, and are consecrated to God.

Through the *anointing with the holy chrism,* the oil that was used to consecrate kings, priests, and prophets, we recognize that the newborn creature is like a king; the infant is no one's subject, but rather a son or daughter; not a servant, but a *priest* in full communion with the Father and with Jesus Christ, the Supreme Priest. Therefore the newborn is capable, through the gifts of the Holy Spirit, of properly worshiping God; the newborn is a *prophet,* a custodian of the Word of God, made to know truth and bear witness to it.

Every pastoral, sacerdotal, and prophetic ministry of the church is in the service of royalty (freedom), of priesthood (holiness), and of prophecy (truth). Without exception, these qualities are shared by all those who are baptized.

The *lit candle* is a symbol of Christ, who is Life and Light. The new life is bright, and the body of the baptized infant is a reflection of God on earth, as the words of St. Paul tell us: "And all of us, with unveiled faces seeing the glory of the Lord as though reflected in a mirror, are being transformed into the same image from one degree of glory to another; for this comes from the Lord, the Spirit" (2 Cor. 3:18).

We are called to be children of the light and to light up the world.

The *white gown* is the visible image of our body that has been born anew because it is dressed in Christ.

Finally, the sign of *Ephphatha*. The priest touches our ears that they may be always open to the word of Jesus; he touches our lips, that we may become capable of expressing this word and professing our faith.

Just like a seed

When I am born there is within me, "like a kernel," my whole life, which has yet to grow and develop.

Baptism is like a seed, the DNA of a new life. Like a seed, it must grow and be nourished; it must be protected from wounds, atrophy, tumors.

All of this shall come about by listening to the word and passing through the other sacraments that accompany the life of the body.

The word of growth

Confirmation is first and foremost the word of growth. It is a sacrament that confirms baptism; therefore, it is appropriately given in the teenage years. It confirms that we are children of the Father. As the Spirit confirms this call to be children of God, it gives us the power to proclaim the Gospel to the world and the strength and the joy to speak boldly of the Resurrected Jesus to an often-indifferent society.

It permits us to continue on our Christian path that began with baptism.

The laying on of hands, which is part of the rite of confirmation, is a gesture of blessing, the transmission of a gift that says, "I make you a participant in the gifts of the Holy Spirit so that having understood the extraordinary grace of baptism, you may commit yourself to your brothers and sisters, placing yourself in their service as Jesus did, who came into the world to serve, not to be served."

The sacrament of confirmation enables us to be responsible collaborators in building the Christian community.

The word of resurrection

Another word that accompanies life is the sacrament of *reconciliation* or *confession;* we ought to consider it as the constant baptism of life.

When we go astray, reconciliation makes us relive the truth of the word, because to sin means to miss the target, to lose our final destination, to deviate from the condition of being a son or daughter, to separate our body from the body of the Lord, from the body of Jesus as the highest gift of love. The word of reconciliation gives us new life.

Eucharist, the word of nourishment

Though our body is not life, it has life, which it sustains with food.

After breathing, eating is our primary need. We can eat alone, from a bowl or a plate, or we can eat as a gesture of interaction, of sharing. Children and siblings eat at the same table because they share the same life. Even the baby takes its first food, milk, in communion with its mother. Unless food is a sharing of life, it cannot satisfy.

We are what we eat. We live and assimilate whatever we put inside our body.

We eat with our mouth, with our five senses that are the five channels through which we interact with the world; we eat with our mind and with our heart. Human nourishment is always linked to a relationship. For aren't anorexia and bulimia forms of eating that lack all relationality?

The Eucharist as food

The Eucharist is the *word of the body* as it nourishes itself, as it eats; it is the word that makes each individual story into a fulfillment of filial and fraternal love.

Unlike food that is assimilated and transformed in our body, in the Eucharist it is Jesus who assimilates us, conforms us to him, to his gift of love for us on the cross. The Eucharist gives meaning to everything, adding a word of thanksgiving.

As we nourish ourselves with the Eucharist, we also learn to live soberly, a result of love, not apathy, for love becomes the only absolute end that reduces everything else to a means. Thus, all human appetites must be satisfied only insofar as they are useful to that end. Love's word regulates our hunger for food, our hunger of the senses, of our minds and our hearts.

Truly, the Eucharist is the word of all our human existence: through it, the realm of necessity is made free, circumscribed by love that is given and received.

Finally, it is a living communion with Being and with all beings, the setting where all creatures and their stories pass from the sixth to the seventh day of creation, with God all in all.

Comfort for our journey

In the Eucharist, we celebrate in advance our final destination; we receive the food for our daily journey. My daily life with all its interrelatonships, my body and all its acts, are called to live in the Eucharist.

Like Jesus

Jesus left us the task of repeating, in memory of him, his very act of offering his life in sacrifice for us.

"He took the bread": bread is life. More than just wheat, which is simply from nature, bread is also culture. I must accept what I have, what I am, and what I am becoming. Not like Adam, who became master of nature, but like the Son, Jesus, who received all.

"He turned his eyes to heaven and blessed": I must learn to accept a gift and turn my eyes toward the Source of all gifts, rejoicing at every gift in the love of the Giver. Every fragment, every crumb is a sign of Our Father's infinite love. I live and receive the Spirit; I am the child of God in every reality.

"He broke the bread and gave it": Jesus the Son received a sign of his father's love; he responded with equal love, even unto the cross, sharing the gift with his brothers and sisters. Love, the life that was given to him, was not barren; it flowered again in love. Like a son he received, yet like his Father's equal he gives to us, to humanity. Thus, the words of Paul are completely fulfilled: "The Lord is for the body" (1 Cor. 6:13).

Caravaggio (1573–1610). Supper at Emmaus. National Gallery,
London, Great Britain. Courtesy: Nimatalla/Art Resource, NY

The true Jubilee

How many times in these past twenty years have I celebrated the Eucharist, carrying the monstrance with the consecrated bread through the streets of the city, in the procession for the feast of Corpus Christi.

How many times have I contemplated Jesus the Eucharist and felt a shiver of fear and a renewed emotion in seeing him weak and defenseless!

The Eucharist is the life of Jesus for us. Jesus is everything to us. He is the one who shows us the face of the Father. The Eucharist makes us one in Christ; it is the foundation of charity that St. Paul glowingly speaks of (1 Cor. 13). The Eucharist proclaims the coming of redemption—the explosion, the outburst of God's love for humanity that culminated in the death and resurrection of Christ.

In sum, the Eucharist is the true Jubilee, the heart of the two-thousand-year Jubilee, when we celebrate the second millennium of the Word Incarnate, the Son of God who was made flesh.

The message of the Mass

We will never finish speaking about the sacrament of the Eucharist because we can never fully express the bounty and wealth of this mystery. In each Mass, we enter into contact with all of God's mystery.

The Eucharist teaches us again and again to treat our body like the temple of God, nourished by God and inhabited and transformed by Jesus. It is a most precious setting where the body comes to appreciate its dynamic condition.

The Eucharist is a powerful message for the men and women of today who are tempted to believe that they have been forsaken, that they are alone, men and women who are afraid of sharing, of letting others into their lives, who refuse to promote life.

In essence, the Eucharist says to them: "Trust me, for I have given my life to you, even dying on the cross for you. Trust me, for I want to nourish you with my flesh. I want to make of your body my house. I want to share your existence and make you partake of my resurrection. You must not feel alone, because I am here with you. I can give meaning to your search, to your restlessness. Turn your sadness into joy and your lonesomeness into communion with your brothers and sisters."

Recognizing the body of the Lord

Being able to recognize the body of the Lord in the poor, plain signs of his appearance is a great grace.

We recognize him not just in the sacramental signs of the bread and the wine, but also in the face of the little ones, in the lowest social outcasts. We recognize him beyond the confines of our Christian communities, beyond the murkiness of so many difficult situations in which so many of our brothers and sisters live in desolation.

To believe in the Eucharist is the essence of Christian faith. To believe means precisely to recognize in the sacramental signs the body of the Lord who nourishes us so that our eyes may be opened and may see him near us and around us. This is why a prolonged adoration of the Eucharist can nourish our spirit, increasing our knowledge of Jesus and of his gift.

The true fruit of the Eucharist

The proper fruit of the Eucharist is charity, the gift of our life to others. Besides making Jesus present to be worshiped and consumed, the Eucharist fills our hearts with the dynamism of love, even unto the cross. It fills us with the Holy Spirit, which is a loving force that unites the Christian community and expands it to include the whole world.

While in confirmation we receive the Spirit so that we may bear witness, reinforcing and complementing our consecration in baptism, in the Eucharist we accept the gift of the Spirit as the fire of charity.

The word in holy orders

To become a priest is a gift from heaven, just like the Eucharist, just like the Word of God, just like Jesus.

The specific word of the sacrament of *holy orders* is that of priestly service.

The gift the priests receive empowers them to be deputies and continue the mission of Jesus, loving the church as he loved it, giving themselves to the people just as he gave of himself.

Ordained ministers serve the faithful by helping them to form that royal people, that holy nation, that spiritual temple whose foundation was laid at the time of baptism.

This service is expressed in the proclamation of the Gospel, the celebration of the Eucharist, the administration of the sacraments, the promotion of charity, the example of personal consecration. It is expressed in the prayers of praise and intercession, so that the Christian communities may be nourished by the Word of God and by the eucharistic body of Christ, and may live holy lives.

There is no church without priests; similarly, there

is no church without the Word of God, without the Eucharist, without the sacraments. Nor are there priests without the church, without Christian communities.

Holy orders keeps the body of the church together, and we must always beseech God for this grace.

The word of love between man and woman—marriage

Just as baptism empowers us to recognize the call to become children of God in Christ, so the sacrament of marriage empowers a man and a woman to recognize the loving word that unites them in one flesh. "Therefore a man leaves his father and mother and clings to his wife, and they become one flesh" (Gen. 2:24).

The truth of marriage

At the origin of every marriage is God. God is the author because by creating man and woman God inscribed in their hearts the capacity and the responsibility to love and to share.

Thus, marriage was in God's design from the very beginning: it is an underlying, constitutive, primary reality linked to the overall divine plan that is transmitted through Jesus and fulfilled in him and in the church.

The mystery of creation and the covenant between God and humankind help us to grasp the full value of the gift a man and a woman give to each other when they enter into faithful marriage. By the same token, and conversely, this reciprocal conjugal gift helps us to understand the mystery of creation and of the covenant.

Sacramental grace

Instituted by God as a sacrament, marriage empowers the Christian spouses with the mystery of fidelity, which is an attribute of God's love. They partake of God's irrevocable will to communicate with humankind. It makes them capable of loving each other as Christ loved and loves the church.

Marriage is the "great mystery" of which St. Paul speaks in his Letter to the Ephesians (5:22–23), and it is a *trace* insofar as it is an echo of the love of Christ and conforms us to him.

Through the power of this sacrament, the Spirit of Jesus received in the gift of baptism gradually brings the spouses closer to Jesus, accompanies them throughout their lives, and makes them real, visible signs of Christ's total, unique, and fruitful love.

A *path to holiness*

Truly, Christian marriage is a reality linked to Jesus and the reign of God. It is the couple's own path toward holiness, the setting where they follow and imitate Christ, their way of following in his footsteps.

This transcendental aspect of marriage, though, does not diminish the value of married life and its substance. On the contrary, it helps the spouses to open themselves to what is final and absolute; it helps them to follow the path that leads to communion with God in Christ, the final, redeeming shores of all human experience.

A *gift to be put into practice every day*

From the very moment of the marriage ceremony, this sacrament is a gift to be discovered and put into practice again and again, day after day.

In all these years, I was fortunate to meet and get to know many Christian couples who told me of their experiences. Therefore, I can affirm that praying together, and in particular receiving the Eucharist together on Sundays, making important decisions together, and sharing the difficult moments that are part and parcel of married life, can contribute to making of marriage a *communication of grace*. All this nourishes and reinforces their awareness of being custodians of a gift, a power, a promise, a light that lights up the way, a mission that surrounds them and sustains them.

Thus, each couple is given the tools to persevere, together with the help of God, to make their life into a work of art that reflects God's union with humankind and Christ's union with the church.

"Not by bread alone . . . "

I often think of an enlightening verse from Deuteronomy (8:3) spoken by Jesus: "Man does not live by bread alone, but by every word that comes from the mouth of God" (Matt. 4:4).

The reference here is to different levels of bodily reality. The *biological* level is that of the body as an organic, primordial reality that is concerned with nourishment, sexuality, and reproduction. At the *human* level, nourishment becomes conviviality, and sexuality is expanded to include friendship between man and woman, marital alliance, education of children, and the family as the building block of society. Finally, the *level of gift, of grace*, includes the two preceding levels, but here the humanized body is guided, moved by the Spirit. Nourishment has now become the Eucharist—the sacred conviviality of the human being with God and other human beings. Instead of merely a conjugal matter, sexuality has now become a sacrament, the spiritual union of man and woman in the context of Christ's love and friendship, a building block of the church, of the multitude of people who shall be redeemed.

By repeating the verse "not by bread alone...," Jesus links life's primordial dynamism to the ultimate dynamism of the gift.

Marriage crisis

Marriage is in a serious state of crisis, including marriages that were celebrated in church.

In this respect, marriage is like a comb where all the knots of society, all the typical contradictions of the society in which we live come together.

Nothing can any longer be taken for granted in marriage. Even the time the couple spends together is threatened by a multitude of other duties and activities!

We are conditioned by the culture that surrounds us and by our jobs, and both have a tendency to fragment. Today, a couple no longer stays together just because the law commands it. The prevailing mentality is one where choices are made "on a temporary basis," not permanently.

Overcoming the crisis

Marriage can survive, provided it is supported by an intelligent, deep, loving relationship that can foster a favorable environment.

The couple must learn to make free, responsible choices; they must also make an ongoing effort to counteract the pressures to separate. A couple needs time for privacy and quiet as well, in order to communicate and to grow together, for it is at such times that they learn to accept each other, to come to terms with their differences, to dialogue, to respect each other, and to share their experiences. Finally, the couple needs the support of other families, meeting together in groups that have the same Christian outlook on marriage.

Fertility

Fertility is participation in the mystery of God as the source of life, in the mystery of the love of the Trinity.

There was a time when society looked at fertility as a blessing, even economically, and still now there is a deep feeling that love between a man and a woman ushers in a new life, a new love.

A child is proof of the fruitfulness of this love, but to live and to grow properly children need the continued renewal of their parents' giving of themselves that initially gave them life.

A love that chooses deliberately to be sterile is not true love; it is double selfishness. And yet Western society keeps growing more and more sterile, increasingly afraid to bring new lives into the world.

In this context, rediscovering the authentic meaning of procreation and responsible parenthood becomes a critical priority. Bringing children into the world can reinforce a sense of what it means to be human that we are at risk of losing. It can provide hope for the future, giving us the courage and serenity to live in the present.

A place where values are carried on

The family is the first place where values are lived and transmitted. Feeding and educating children are not enough, for children demand love. They ask for meaning and values; they want to see that it's possible to live a life of values with ease and joy.

Accepting the challenge

The "sanctity" of marriage is definitely more difficult to achieve today, but where it does exist, it is more clearly visible.

Once more, I would like to invite Christian couples to accept a challenge.

The challenge is that true married love, that love which is a visible sign of God's love for humanity, is not only beautiful but can also exist and thrive in a society that tends to isolate and to create conformity. It is a sort of prophetic provocation, something that has value, that is lasting, a love covenant that is stronger than any other bond because it is a beacon of God's eternal sun.

The charism of virginity

Living a celibate life, the life of a virgin, dedicating it to God's reign, gives us a foretaste of the final reality.

It is a feasible choice, provided we treat it as a special gift from God to one person that benefits everyone, an extraordinary path, an anticipation of the destiny of all our bodies, which is *to be for God*.

Virginity and marriage

Virginity anticipates the true meaning of Christian marriage, which is that of a body freely given to love and to serve. Virginity represents a dynamism of grace and of submission to Christ, our only Lord, of growth in passionate love for him: this also is an integral part of the dynamism of marriage.

From this point of view, the church needs the charism of celibates to help couples live their own union, like a spice that stimulates their journey.

In turn, marriage can be proof of how virginity ought to be lived, as love expressed with all of one's heart and life, with all of one's strength and intelligence; it is the joy of serving and of giving oneself.

At the feet of Jesus

Rather than a sacrifice, virginity is one form of conjugal reality insofar as it defines itself in relation to Jesus, as a reciprocal, freely given act: it is putting oneself at the feet of Jesus. Thus, virginity points to the mystery of the person, even the mystery of the Trinity: the Father is the one who is in relation to the Son; the Son is the one who is in relation to the Father; the Spirit is the one who is in relation to the Father and the Son.

Taking possession of the value of virginity

Making the value of virginity one's own is a grace given by the Holy Spirit; it is an inner strength.

The choice to be celibate is not the result of a rational argument. Jesus says: "For there are eunuchs who have been so from birth, and there are eunuchs who have been made eunuchs by others, and there are eunuchs who have made themselves eunuchs for the sake of the kingdom of heaven. Let anyone accept this who can" (Matt. 19:12).

A rigorous analysis of the first two chapters of Genesis might lead us to believe that the marital relationship is the only possible one within the order of the creator God. By revealing to us the final situation of the believer, however, the situation that is closest to God, Jesus helps us to understand that in Genesis 1:27—"in the image of God he created them; male and female he created them"—the dynamics of virginity are also stressed.

The Crucified Spouse

Choosing to be celibate for God's reign—choosing to be alone with Christ—is an unusual state, a choice that is valid within the framework of the redemption that Christ, the crucified Spouse, has achieved for us. The Spirit gives to man or woman the grace of being united with Jesus in a privileged way, in a way that can fulfill one's life.

A precious presence

In addition to bearing witness to married couples on the authentic meaning of marriage, the charism of virginity also shows those who by reason of birth, environment, or other circumstances could not find a companion, that their lives can still be fulfilling.

"Come, Lord Jesus!"

Every time I read the following words of St. Paul I am touched by them: "The appointed time has grown short" and "the present form of this world is passing away" (1 Cor. 7:29, 31).

These words make me better understand that *love is for everyone, and lives eternally,* and I rejoice at this truth.

Virginity, which announces the future resurrection and the glory of God's reign, has a central place in the church and in humanity, as it makes its own the mysterious cry, the lovely invocation "Amen. Come, Lord Jesus!" (Rev. 22:20).

A word that gives meaning to illness

The sacrament of the anointing of the sick is not only for those who are about to die, as people often believe. It was instituted for all those who are seriously ill.

The "fracturing" of the body

Illness attacks the body and upsets its meaning.

Whereas interacting, loving, eating, give us a feeling of satisfaction—the coincidence between need or desire and its gratification—illness creates a fracture because it contradicts and prevents that to which I aspire.

It is an experience of displeasure, of ill-being, of failure, that breaks up the spontaneous, meaningful order of life.

This is why in addition to medical care, the sick person looks for comfort and company and seeks help in understanding the meaning of this new situation.

The grace of the Resurrected One

The anointing of the sick confers the grace of the Resurrected One. Christ makes my sick body his own, removes the pain, and restores it to spiritual and physical health, strengthening and comforting me. He lovingly forgives my sins and gives me to understand the meaning of pain in the light of his Passion, with which he unites me.

Thus, in this sacrament, Jesus continues to address the sick as he did when he was on earth, and as he enjoined his disciples: "Cure the sick who are there, and say to them, 'the kingdom of God has come near to you' " (Luke 10:9).

Faith's reply

Anointing the sick is not a magical act. It requires faith, just like the other sacraments.

Sick persons who place themselves in the powerful hands of God will be able to overcome the fears and temptations that prey on those who are in pain. They will find serenity and inner peace; they will feel encouraged to hope in recovery and at the same time will accept all the possible outcomes of their illness.

Toward the "dies natalis"

The sacrament of the anointing of the sick also prepares us for death, whether it be near or far, not specifically, but simply because of the fact that illness, serious illness especially, is a harbinger of death.

I would hope that the Spirit I receive in this sacrament would help me and others to see death as it truly is, as the final fulfillment of baptism, when we shall enter our true life as children of God and brothers and sisters of each other.

Jesus is the first man who lived death as an act of communion. He put himself in the hands of men just as he put himself in the hands of his Father, living that negative condition as an act of giving himself to others and to the Other. The body of Jesus incarnates even unto death the word of love.

Our death, anticipated by the many "fractures" of our body, is not a point of arrival but a passage, a very narrow passage that allows us, as new persons, to be born. It is the *dies natalis* when our body fulfills its word, the word of the Son in whom and for whom we were created.

Thus, illness reveals what is *human,* and death reveals what is *divine.*

THE RESURRECTION
OF THE BODY

◆

*The Resurrection of Christ is like the first erup-
tion of a volcano, revealing, as it does, that the
fire of God is already burning within the world,
and will lead everything back to the heat of
its light.*   —Karl Rahner

NOTHING IS MORE COMFORTING than knowing that our body will be reborn and that our separation from those we love is not permanent.

The first desire

Human beings are *humus*. We come from the earth and to the earth we shall return. We are mortal and know it, and this makes us human.

We return to the earth like a seed fallen from a plant; we return to the place whence we came, as a promise of life.

Resurrection is not simply putting life back into a corpse, which then starts living anew, as mortal as it was before. Instead, it is the fullness of happiness and of life—for there is no happiness without life—to which we have always aspired.

It is the fulfillment of our first desire, that of becoming God-like (see Gen. 3:5), a desire that was purified, ordained, and achieved by God in Christ.

All human culture is a sort of machine tending to overcome its limitations. Within ourselves we experience the anxiety of freeing ourselves of the final limitation, so that we may live an existence free from the mortgage of death.

The beginning of universal resurrection

Resurrection, the central tenet of Christian faith, has to do with the *body* and is based on the experience of the resurrected Christ. His resurrection and ours are so intimately joined that one cannot be true without the other.

In fact, Jesus was born again *for us;* this is the beginning of the universal resurrection of the dead.

The whole of history is seen as a travail that gives birth to the new creature. Creation itself waits impatiently, "groaning in labor pains until now," waiting to be born in the glory of the children of God and the redemption of the body (see Rom. 8:19–24).

This, of course, has nothing to do with the theory of reincarnation that rejects the resurrection of the body because it believes the body is a burden to be discarded.

Easter morning

On Easter morning, the head, Jesus Christ, revealed himself. Then the body followed, and we are the body. He was the first to live a life that extends beyond death, the firstborn among many siblings, the firstborn among those who are resurrected from the dead.

Resurrection is the beauty of God given to humankind and, through it, to all creation: it is the new heaven and the new earth that Isaiah (65:17) gazed at, where everything has the wonder of an eternal morning, without sunset ever, an endless fountain of joy.

Finally, restless humankind, which finds—in the words of Ecclesiastes—that "nothing is new under the sun" (1:9) can discover the amazing truth we had been seeking so long.

It is a "vision" that goes beyond our imagination, but it is also the secret dream of our hearts.

Here and now

Thanks to the death and resurrection of Jesus, eternity—the new, definitive life—has already entered my life.

I live eternity here and now, in my indestructible acts of love, faithfulness, forgiveness, friendship, honesty, and responsible freedom. Through these acts, I mysteriously transcend time and reach eternity,

107

insofar as I trust myself to the life and the eternity of the Crucified One who overcame death.

I rejoice in thinking that I can redeem the anguish of time, the history of my body, through acts of dedication that have a lasting value, a value that is safeguarded by the fullness of the resurrected body of Christ.

I rejoice in thinking that each word I speak as I pray is like a stone thrown into eternity that helps to build the eternal house.

Transfiguration and transformation in God

Of course, we cannot imagine the resurrection of our body, just as we cannot depict light or life, intelligence or love.

We do know, however, that resurrection is the source of all our representations, as well as all imagined reality. This is why we *talk* about it like something that gives meaning to our existence as men and women. It is the Word that communicates the mystery to us.

My body becomes like a word of acceptance; lifeless dust comes to life in the seed that springs from it.

For what is a plant if not an ensemble of elements

of the earth and the sky, "informed" by the genetic code, by the vital word of the buried seed? And what is an animal if not the plant or whatever else it eats, "informed" by its unique code? And what are human beings if not what we assimilate? Everywhere, everything is always being transformed and transfigured; it changes shape and figure according to the specific code it receives from life.

Love is God's life code; it is what instructs and informs life. If I listen to God's Word, little by little I am transformed and transfigured into God, and with the resurrection of the body, I will share in God's life.

Thus, my body is not just a tool for listening and echoing the Word: it is the Word that gives it life.

"The Word became flesh" (John 1:14)

My earthly body will receive as a vital principle the Spirit of God and will be fully penetrated by the Holy Spirit.

From the moment that Christ, the Father's Eternal Word, became flesh, so my flesh will become divine.

The event of the Incarnation, the Son of God made flesh, proclaims that our mortal bodies are destined to be raised again.

"I am the resurrection and the life. Those who

believe in me, even though they die, will live, and everyone who lives and believes in me will never die" (John 11:25–26).

As to the Eucharist, Jesus said: "Those who eat my flesh...I will raise them up on the last day" (John 6:54).

The story of the Transfiguration

To better understand our body's destiny, I would like first of all to recount the story of Jesus' Transfiguration.

Not knowing how to describe the glory of the body of Jesus, Luke writes that his clothes became full of light, dazzling white, and "the appearance of his face changed" (Luke 9:29), shining with a beauty that was "other" than ordinary beauty: it was the beauty of God, of the holy.

What is important to stress here is that during his natural life, the body of Jesus revealed his hidden glory, an anticipated reverberation of the final glory that was to be manifested in his resurrection.

The divine light is manifested in our body throughout our journey, and not simply at the end of it, for all our life is a slow, gradual journey of illumination that increasingly lights up our days.

"Listen to him!"

A voice from heaven offers us the principle of this illumination: "Listen to him!" (Luke 9:35).

By listening to him who is the Word made flesh, who fully lived the injunction to love, all flesh participates in his glory.

The face of the Father that we are all seeking as the light of our face and that no one can see is the face of the Son and of all those who, by listening, become his brothers and sisters.

Says John: "The hour is coming and is now here, when the dead will hear the voice of the Son of God, and those who hear will live" (John 5:25); and again, "We know that we have passed from death to life because we love one another" (1 John 3:14).

The eternal life that will fully flourish in the future has already been given to us: it is the *quality of life* of those who listen to the word of the Son and who live like brothers and sisters.

It is the experience, also lived by St. Paul, that made him say, "And all of us, with unveiled faces, seeing the glory of the Lord as though reflected in a mirror, are being transformed into the same image from one degree of glory to another" (see 2 Cor. 3:18).

A comforting truth

Though when I am born I have a certain face that I inherited, once I am grown I have the face that I've tried to build for myself. My face is like an outline of the sorrows and the joys I have experienced, of my slavery and my freedom, of my selfishness and my love. My face displays the darkness or the light of the words that were sown and cultivated in my heart.

Understanding that our existence is a process of transfiguration in which we become gradually truer to the image of the Son of God is a great comfort.

Giotto's frescoes

Giotto depicts the story of the Transfiguration of Jesus in a lovely fresco: two splendid icons that open up the horizon of indescribable and unfathomable realities.

The capture of Jesus

Those who are fortunate enough to visit the Scrovegni Chapel in Padua—a veritable jewel—will find, approximately midway on the right-hand wall of the nave, the fresco that depicts Jesus being arrested in the Garden of Gethsemane after the long night spent in prayer.

The sullen sky is broken by a multitude of poles, clubs, and spears, and the two torches do not give enough light.

In the center, surrounded by a black background of faceless heads is a kiss: the kiss of Judas, whose mantle is wrapped around Jesus and under which we perceive the arms that are seizing him. It is the agreed-upon "sign" that marks him who must be captured and killed. The blurred background of excited people moving about provides a strong contrast to the two motionless central bodies enclosed in a mortal embrace.

Mary Magdalene meets the Resurrected One

On the left wall, facing that fresco, is the fresco of Mary Magdalene and the Resurrected Jesus, a theme that Giotto repeated in the Lower Basilica of Assisi.

Here the sky is polished, filled with a mysterious cerulean blue and closed below by a sharply delineated horizon filled with plants and shrubs. To the left, the tomb to which Judas' embrace had led Jesus stands empty. Two angels, sitting on it, point to Jesus; the guards below are sleeping a death-like sleep.

113

Giotto di Bondone (1266–1336). *The Kiss of Judas.* Scrovegni Chapel, Padua, Italy. Courtesy: Alinari/Art Resource, NY

Giotto di Bondone (1266–1336). *Noli me tangere* (Christ Appearing to Mary Magdalene). Scrovegni Chapel, Padua, Italy. Courtesy: Alinari/Art Resource, NY

In the center is Magdalene: she turns her shoulders to the tomb and reaches toward Jesus, who seems to be a flower blossoming in her open arms.

Magdalene is dressed in red, Jesus in white and gold, like the rising sun.

The astonished, standstill quality of everything else in the fresco—sky and horizon, plants and sepulcher, angels and guards—highlights even more intensely the dynamism of this encounter.

Two contrasting movements

The Resurrected One has two contrasting movements: one toward Mary, almost pulling her toward him and away from the tomb; the other in the opposite direction, leading her beyond the very frame of the painting, toward the infinite horizon from which a wind blows the white pennant that flutters against the clear sky.

These two movements symbolize the double destiny of the human body.

They represent, respectively, the two types of relationships that we have with the body of the other and with the reality of the Other: our attempt to enclose it and suffocate it, or our openness to it, accepting it and being swept toward the light. They are two opposite words that inform our body: death and life. The second does not ignore the first, but comes after it.

My name

I think that in these frescoes Giotto was inspired by the Gospel of John, where the two scenes—of Judas and of Mary Magdalene—are ideally parallel scenes. They are united by the question Jesus asks of the guards escorting Judas and of the woman crying near the tomb: "Whom are you looking for?" and "Woman, why are you weeping? Whom are you looking for?" (John 18:4, 7; 20:15). Mary was crying because she had not found the body of Jesus.

The embrace takes place after the Resurrected One has manifested himself. He was already present, but she did not recognize him, even though she did know him! She thought he was the gardener.

She finally sees him when he speaks her name: "Mary!" Then she recognizes in that face her beloved, her life, and she is swept away from the tomb and carried with him toward the light that goes beyond what can be represented.

One simple word sufficed to transform her completely, from mourning to ecstasy.

Thus I am transfigured when the Other, the one who loves me with eternal love, utters my name, tells me who I am, and gives me my identity.

My name always comes from another and, in the final instance, from the Other. In one simple word, he tells me what I am and what the other is.

This total, reciprocal belonging to Life is the victory over death: it is resurrection.

EPILOGUE

The ineffable dream of God who is given to us in Jesus before every human hope or expectation, who loves us and freely forgives us, is fulfilled through the responsible lives of men and women who live as sons and daughters of the Father and as brothers and sisters.

It is the dream that everything shall return to the Trinity, from which everything originates and to which everything tends.

It is the dream inscribed in creation: that nothing that is good and beautiful and desirable shall be lost.

Even for those who stubbornly refuse God, who is Love—but how can someone who has known love reject it?—the Resurrected One lets us hope against all hope that God's mercy shall conquer all resistance.

Like the Word, who at the beginning was with the Father, took on our human body and is now again with God, we dare to hope that one day we shall all with our bodies be with God in God's light and in God's life.

But all of this will come about through our presenting our bodies as gifts of love, as absolute, earnest gifts, without regrets or cheapening of our love.